Hero Veterans vs. the Veterans Administration

Clint Dean

authorHOUSE®

AuthorHouse™
1663 Liberty Drive
Bloomington, IN 47403
www.authorhouse.com
Phone: 1-800-839-8640

Published by AuthorHouse 07/20/2012

ISBN: 978-1-4772-4406-7 (sc)
ISBN: 978-1-4772-4407-4 (e)

Library of Congress Control Number: 2012913004

ACKNOWLEDGEMENT

I WANT TO Thank my Lord, for the many times he has diverted the bullets. Also, my fellow service members, for all of their sacrifices.

To all who buy and read this book, it is intended to educate, relate and plead for help from the peoples of this great nation;

THE UNITED STATES OF AMERICA

FOR ALL OF OUR ENDURING AND FALLEN FELLOW VETERANS.
ESPICIALLY TO THOSE WHO MADE THE ULTIMATE SACRIFICE THEIR LIFE

MY AMAZING WIFE
THEIR HOURS SPENT FOR THIS. SHE HAS BEEN A ROCK FOR ME. LOVE
HER INTENSELY

CONTENTS

CHAPTER ONE

Before I begin, I must first, include an understanding of the Veterans Administration(hereafter-VA), By Law, established by an Act Of Congress, and since 1933, when the VA, was established, Congress, has continually passed laws that prevent any outside review through the Courts, or Lawsuits against VA, decisions.

This leaves Veterans completely at the mercy of the VA. Its decisions are final. I personally feel this is no more than dictatorship, and a direct ACT, by Congress, to order into combat, our men and women to get wounded, loss of life and limbs, then when the Veteran, has served his/her purpose, when you apply for benefits and compensation, you become incumbent upon the mercy of The Veterans Administration. Please don't think because of the standards they establish and press release's they care. The VA does not!

Title 38 U.S.C. Sec. 211 (a) (1970), Congress expressed and re-emphasized "it's clear intent that the EXEMTION from judicial review…BE INCLUSIVE!!

I wonder why. They use us Vets, for War, and then discard us as so much trash. The VA is the most BEAUCRATIC agency of the US Government. I have been in claims, Remands, US Court of Appeals for Veteran claims And the VA, does what it wants when it wants and how it desires, without fear of reprisal or review. This has and is ongoing for over 20 years, in my case.

The question thusly remains why Congress does, order you into Combat, then disregard your health and wellbeing. Interesting isn't it!!! The President of the United States, issues the order, but; congress authorizes and funds the war. I feel as though this was initially set into place when the VA, was initially created because Congress at that time enacted the law to protect the VA, from the Court's review. Many veterans have tried and many continue today, to sue the VA, and the VA, is a machine that can drive the ordinary person broke. It's very good at delays. Most Court decisions are denied, because of the Congressional Act, of NOT SUBJECT TO THE JUDICIAL REVIEW, provision established by Congress.

When you file a claim, you must claim the specific fact, the VA, will not tell you if you have a right to claim anything else. They won't volunteer any information. Rather than assist, get ready for the rule, law, facts, sub part a to appendix a, to subpart, it goes on and on. I found quite by accident several illnesses that I had, and by provisions and laws of the VA, were compensation issues. However; upon all the occasions the VA, has reviewed or supposedly reviewed my medical records, they never mentioned this. The Veteran Claims Assistance Act; states in part; it is the duty of the VA, to assist the veteran in perfecting a claim. Again, that is what I consider "propaganda on behalf of the VA". The numerous press releases sound good, but; rarely enacted. In May 2012, the VA issued a press release that it was hiring nationwide, 1900 people for the mental health clinics. That is yet to happen. Just another pretty picture. The VA, got caught in testimony before the Veterans committee on veteran affairs, the VA, downplayed the number of daily, monthly suicides of returning veterans, and when the 9th circuit court of appeals issued its decision in California, it cited numerous emails between VA, officials that they had in fact under-reported the numbers. In addition emails surfaced that with all the emphasis on mental health and post-traumatic stress syndrome, VA, sent several regional offices notice that they were APPROVING TOO MANY PTSD CLAIMS. Otherwise deny them so they stay in appeals for untold number of years. The veteran while on appeal cannot get care thru the VA, bringing another burden upon the veteran and the public health care system. Creating more reasons for the increase in the number of suicides. Besides, in the VA, if you are going to commit suicide, do it between 8am and 4pm, the VA, will not assist you after hours. This may be construed as an out of context statement, but; it's the truth.

The VA, also, does not have handouts or briefings to service members departing the service to help and assist in the claims process. You are on your own. Get ready!!!!!

Vets, getting out don't know to obtain copies of their personnel records, especially copies of their record of assignments and injuries treated while in service. Therefore when a vet first files his/her claim, it will take many months or more, to obtain from the records center. I f while in the military, you conducted subversive missions, and many did, and your records are sealed, you will never be able to receive medical treatment or benefits. I have personally helped and assisted a vet in the same condition along with a state vet representative, because the Vet was dying. To no Avail. He died. Dr. Gupta, CNN, helped a vet in the same situation, and had a hard time, but; on TV, got the VA, under-secretary to come get the Vets paperwork and get benefits. But; they would not allow them access to the VA building, on TV, they came downstairs and outside to get the papers and walked immediately back inside. Kind of, odd, but; it's just a vet.

In the newspapers, a May 2012, full appeals Court of the 9th CC of appeals, would not uphold the Revamp of the VA, said it was the duty of Congress, ha, good luck with that!!

Ref: Veterans for Common Sense VS Secretary of the VA, Shinseki, 05-07-12, No. 08-16728. You can view online and read a lot about the VA.

When seeing a VA, Doctor, please always remember, should he make a definitive decision and tell you that you suffer from a specific disease, then that doctor, by diagnosis, gives you the right to file a claim. Do you think that will happen?? VA, doctors are trained to avoid that, I think, maybe, more test's etc., is what you will get more often than a specific diagnosis. Especially if it involves a listed disease that VA, associates with tropical diseases.

One should know that the 11 diseases associated and caused by Agent Orange, many are DEADLY, are not shared by the New England Medical journal. Your Doctor by any specialty does not know this. It is only the VA. So, go to VA.Gov, select the Dept. of Veteran affairs website and printout these and take to your doctor, so that he/she, when treating you is WELL aware of these diseases. Many diseases are linked and are Leukemia in various degrees' and forms, Cancers, diabetes, etc.

The blood test for Agent Orange exposure only the VA does. If you ask any lab tech they look thru their book, and all that I have ask, has found none. Your blood level containing DIOXEN IS IMPORTANT.

This Agent Orange shows no outside effects, it eats you from the inside out. Spreads very fast, and is a Killer.IT has a 30 to 50 year incubation period that it lays dormant. The VA, every couple years adds a new disease or two or three. Would really like to know what all it causes, but; just a few at a time, is all you get.

The disease from IRAQ and Afghanistan are just now after 10 years of the first Desert storm debacle, is just now being released. Many Desert storm Vets have been sick, but; when the VA, does not recognize a disease, it isn't happening, no matter how many soldiers, vets, get sick, too bad. Shame on the VA. But; after all it is a government agency and protected by Congress.

I know that with the release of this book, the VA, is going to send the FBI, Secret Service, Dept. of Justice, Iris, and anybody else, to find me, take all my benefits, leave me with no Service Connected benefits, but; hey, someone since 1933, needs to get it told. The VA, and Congress, needs to have their lower extremities expose for what they are, users and abusers. After all, this is America, land of the free, (except those involved with the VA) No other country that I know of treats their Vets like this. You are sent to war, get shot at, risk your life, hear those bullets whizzing by, knowing someone is trying to kill me, and when you survive or you become wounded, can't serve anymore, instead of being treated with respect and dignity, get discarded like trash, ignored, given the runaround, and lastly, NOT ACKNOWLEDGED!!

I have heard people say look at that VA hospital, those Vets have it made free medicine, Doctors etc. You should know that the vast majority of Vets, would gladly trade their VA card for your private insurance.

I must state at this juncture that not all VA employees are bad. Only 10% try, 5% care, the rest, will treat you indignantly, talk down to you, insult you, the two most flagrant instances are you will be greeted with a negative attitude, and the feeling of why bother me. If you get mad at all this treatment on a daily basis, and raise your voice, the VA, police has a goon squad that will run thru the hallways, grab the Vet, and put him out of the facility. They can have an attitude to the Vet, but; hey, if you develop one, you're out the door. They do protect each other. The waits, delays, and scorn you receive are supposed to be taken in stride. Most VA, employees forget, it's the Vet that creates their job, but; is treated as the Vet, is a pain in the butt. Truly so. I have been experiencing this for 20 plus years, and it never stops. Ranting about the delays, the endless hours of waiting, personal conversations, trying to talk to someone, while they keep looking away to view their mobile phone or electronic booklet, is enough to make you boil over, but; one must suck it up, it will never end. If you should ever have the time and occasion to go to a VA Medical Center, get a coke or cup of coffee, and sit out on the patio. Observe the number of people walking from building to building, meeting and talking endlessly, it's not business. After 10 or 20 minutes, you will begin to see the same people walking back, in 10 minutes or so here they come again for a long walk. At my medical center, the same 4 ladies, I watch while having lunch, they walk out to the same building, come back, and in 5 minutes or so, here they go again, this goes on longer than I have time to observe. I attempted to get a question answered, I finally ask the clerk, if she could speak to me direct, by putting her electronic tablet down, she got an attitude, and then her supervisor came out and sounded me off very direct. This is not an isolated happening, most all employees monitor their electronic devices right by their computer or work station. The VA, has many relatives and friends of friends working at each facility, and don't think there is stern supervision. My term for not all, but; the vast majority, is the Veteran, is last, and I'm on paid vacation all the time. I apologize, but; unless you spend time at the VA, you just can't imagine, it always seems, feels, and observing, there is no urgency, a lack of self-drive, and no one to instill that work ethic.

I will begin this paragraph, by saying, here is the starting point where the VA, puts Veterans behind the eight ball for 1 to 5 years, on their initial claim for service connection. It's the dreaded Compensation and Pension Exam. This is well-designed Rouge, a farce, and a set-up.

After a Veteran files a claim for Service Connected Disability, because of war related wounds, the regional Office will order what is called a comp/pen evaluation. These doctors (in most cases a Nurse Practitioner), that doesn't on average work in a unit that see's veterans on a daily appointment schedule. Now, we begin the set-up! No matter what outside Doctor, or VA, doctor is treating you for, medical tests, etc.; most all C/P. examiners will tell you answer yes/no to their questions. Do not elaborate on any question. They watch you're every move, getting on the table, walking in the door, everything. (I was ordered into a wheelchair, but; on a recent c/p, exam, the examiner did not annotate that I was confined to a wheelchair-HOW CONVENIENT!) They will give you a complete exam on the exterior, they might order an x-ray or specific test, they only test your movements, do not look inside you. Agent Orange and Gulf War diseases are from the inside. From this exam and not taking into account what your VA Doctor is treating you for, remembers that doctor, is your primary Care, and has tested you for many things, not the c/p doctor. Wait 2 or 3 days, go to the records release, and request a copy of your c/p exam. I ask you not read it till you get home and sit down. Otherwise you may have an accident from being severely ticked off.

Here is my happening, and I have had many of these, even to achieve the level of 100% service connected. I'm in a VA, doctors 'office and he orders me permanently to a wheelchair-manual. I have diabetic neuropathy to lower extremities, insulin diabetic, 5 shots a day, don't feel cuts or scrapes, four valve heart bypass, six stents, 100% arthritic, one-half my right lung missing from cancer, all agent orange related, no gallbladder. The C/P exam stated and I have Agent Orange infection and many more diseases... I had both lungs no evidence of lung removal, my diabetes was under control, I had all body parts, heart didn't show signs of distress, I had all nerve sensory sensations and feelings, no mention of wheelchair and the doctor said I was fully capable of full time work. Ha, would you hire me-NO. I will begin in chapter two to explain why this happens, the end result of how this impacts you, and the long arduous paperwork WAR begins. I do hope you read on! This is a result of the dreaded comp and pen exam. These are doctors and nurse PR actioners that don't normally work in direct patient care. Wonder why??? This doctor had to call x-ray and get them to recheck the film, sure enough they had me mixed up, and when they put my film on her screen, it presented a different picture but; didn't change her recommendation. I was fully capable of performing daily work with no restrictions. No employer will hire someone who has to check his blood sugar 6 times a day. Take 5 injections daily. Constantly having to drink fluids, because of diabetes, go to the bathroom, every 15 to 30 minutes, have to eat on a schedule of every 2 hours, has to take shots in his spine every 3 months just to be able to move around, do you really think any employer would hire me??? I think the very thought is more than ludicrous. But; this is the VA, in action. Now your claim will be denied and you will have to appeal, now wait for 1 to 3 years. The VA, would be best served to eliminate the comp and Penn, rely on what your VA, doctor has SAID ABOUT YOU, AFTER ALL HE HAS ORDERED YOUR TESTS AND EXAMINED YOU, KNOWS ABOUT YOU. That makes sense doesn't it??? Or, it's a government bureaucratic bundled mess, created to delay. I leave that to personal judgment, I think you know my answer,

To someone that is not a veteran, the frustrations of the VA, system dealt with, is so stressful, it makes combat seem as though you were on a vacation. I mean this literally. With the advent of computer age, electronic communication, one would think the VA, would be in tune with present day society. They being except, have no cause to be efficient. When you have to appeal, your records have to be sent to the board of veteran appeals. My records are 11 folders, huge and thick. So thru the mail it goes, received in Washington, D.C. Then they have to go thru special post office screening, then after about 2 or 3 weeks will finally arrive at the board. Should as the majority of time, your case be remanded back to your regional office, back thru the mail it goes. However, the VA, created this ingenious new glitch, call THE APPEALS MANAGEMENT CENTER. The veterans service groups and all I have spoken with in preparation of this book, will state that this is the utmost in delay tactic put in place. It is another area that stacks up veteran claims, and again 1 to 4 years waiting. This agency is supposed to gather and expedite your remand. A go between of the appeals board and regional office. When you get stuck at this agency. You are sunk. I last year received and split decision. I had two issues on appeal. One part was decided against an entity of the VA, and another part was remanded to the appeals management center for further development. Meanwhile, since the VA, is not automated, while my records are at the appeals mgmt. agency, nothing can be done on the other part of my remand at the regional office, because my records are stuck at the appeals agency. So, part is lying around, I have had one letter from the appeals agency in 14 months. I would like to have both working at the same time. But; since the VA, still works with pencil and paper, not automated, both are lying dormant. Meanwhile my health and compensation for wounds from 50 years ago, are lying around, going nowhere. Great job VA!!!

Since the VA, is and has four separate entities whom do not share information, it seems evident that automation is not a goal or objective of this disorganized agency. Automating would make them more efficient. Why do they not automate?? Perhaps Congress protects them, and they don't have a care in the world. We have fought their war, so who cares now. And that is the main attitude of veterans. It is clear and evident the VA has no concern.

CHAPTER TWO

The Comp/pen continuance. When you get home and read, first you must copy and send a NOD, (Notice of Disagreement to the regional Office), if not they will accept the Doctor's recommendations. All that I stated in the end of chapter 1, the doctor said I could perform daily work and routine.

This is the procedure to which the VA, puts you behind the eight ball. From now on you are continuously disagreeing and attempting to overcome the decision of the Doctor. This is difficult to accomplish. Your claim will more than likely be denied, and the appeal to the Board of Veterans appeals begins. This is time consuming, long drawn out. First file another NOD, wait months for a Statement of the case, type out your objections, document and use C.F.R. title 18, in your response. These two volumes are the VA, laws, rules and procedures. Have a copy of everything from the Va, and your civilian doctor, as well as what happened to you in service. Most Veterans as well as this author, does not trust the VA, when they are working, they see a civilian doctor. Always get a copy and ask the doctor to write you his findings and diagnosis, VA, will consider these. Keep a copy of your notice of disagreement and response to your statement of the case. The Regional Office will instruct you to send to them and a copy they will send of the appeal paper to fill out. Please, I say this from EXPERIENCE<< they will only send to board of veteran appeals, what they feel is pertinent. You, keep a copy, and send the appeal notice and your NOD, plus your response to the statement of the case to the Board. Most likely the Board will rule that there was a procedural error by the Regional Office, and remand it for further development. The Regional Office likes to get rid of case files, and an appeal is right down their alley, you did them a favor. The board will send it to the appeals management center, and get ready because you will be in for a 2 to 3 year delay here. Everyone wants the Appeals mgmt. center to go away, but; it is a delay tactic, intentionally created by the VA. I'm not saying this out of bitterness, it is fact. The Disabled American Vets, American Legion, and many more Service Organizations, will state the same, I'm not the first.

The Board of Appeals is famous for REMANDS, and the regional office knows when they send your file there, it's coming back. The VA, in April 2012, sent out a news release stating how their new program was to eliminate errors, I'm still waiting. Dah!

While your file is in appeal, guess what, you can't file any new claims. Even with computers, they must send your file to the board, then the board sends it to the appeals mgmt. center, while it's there, no new claims can be submitted. Man o live are you seeing a defeat you before it begins(system in place????)

All of the VA, is separate, even though they do have computers. The Health, benefits, regional offices, board of appeals, appeals mgmt. center, all do not share your information. When you see a doctor at the VA, the regional Office will send you a medical release, and then when they get it, they will send to your facility and get a copy. I'm still puzzled even though I wrote that. It's the absolute dumbest thing in modern times, EXCEPT-IT ADDS TO DELAY!!!!!!!..............

Got that figured out! When you see on TV, how the rehab centers at Walter reed Hospital are doing, hey, that is great. When they discharge you and you go to the VA, please don't have a mindset it's the same. You will have nightmares. The most antiquated equipment, archaic methods, I can't become as negative as I would prefer.

The main problem with claims at the regional and other places where you file and appeal IS, hey, they don't hire vets. You would be too sympathetic; people are hired and trained from off the streets. They have no conception of Combat, the stress related with it, and no conception of the military. Not negative, but; a lot are foreign nationals. So, when filing your claim you must be very elementary in your descriptive analysis. You are filing with a non-veteran, non-combat person. They have the VA, guide and you can read it in CFR 18, and you will be floored how the VA, rates claims. I have to be in a wheelchair, but, my neuropathy is only 10% disabling. Now I have a new claim pending because, I need a wheelchair, but; the issue is only 10%, it saves the VA, money. You can spend the rest of your life fighting the issue. They have nothing to lose.

In the VA, budget submission and annual report of expenditures, the VA Secretary, is a Presidential Cabinet Officer. Therefore he has to have Secret service Protection, and Security. Government plane, helicopters, etc. He goes on these nationwide swings to dedicate and re-dedicate VA, centers, go to the hospitals and shake hands with the VETS-what a joke. If you tell him a problem, how long does he retain what you said??? I wouldn't shake his hand, and tell him to leave my bedside. All the money it takes for him to travel, his per diem, and expenses, and the taxpayer expense, he could take care of many veterans. He was relieved of duty as the Chief of Staff of Army. I guess I'll be nice, he had to retire quickly. That was all on national TV, I'm not gossiping.

I guarantee, the VA Secretary, does not stay in Motel 6, or eat at McDonalds.

If after all that, I hope you don't do as many vets do, drop out. This is designed to get you to drop out. The many decisions and legalities, is overwhelming. I'm a former paralegal, so I do research, but; to a person who is not familiar with legal issues, it will and has caused many veterans to give up and drop out. The VA, is good at quoting the United States Code, and Title 18 of the federal Regulations to a veteran. But, all the attempts by veteran service organizations have the courts order a revamp of the VA, cannot happen because of the laws established by congress to protect the VA.

Imagine how I felt, I complained of a sharp pain just below my right breast. The doctor ordered a non-dye cat scan. It was clear. Had I not doubled checked, I would not have been here today. As most all vets, either, if working they have insurance, and are on their spouse's insurance, so as to receive an outside doctors care. t. I went to see my private Oncologist. He performed a cat scan, and lord and behold I had stage one, almost stage two lung cancer. I told him the VA, had just done a scan it was clear, that cancer popped up quick. He seriously looked at me and said "it has been there and is almost stage two."

Had I relied on the VA, I would be dead right now-right. This why so many Vets, go to civilian doctors as well. Since there is no requirement for a VA, doctor to have malpractice insurance, he doesn't need it, because he is protected by Congress. Can't sue. Can't challenge his medical license, nothing. And, if an M.D., works for the VA, he is not doing it out of being patriotic, they only pay in the vicinity of $80K, to $100k plus. An M.D. can make that in three months. Most all are again, of foreign origin. Not negative, but; the truth. All va doctors, nurses, and professional occupations that require a license, guess what, can work anywhere in the United States. Have no license in any particular state, does not have to comply with state standards. They work for "UNCLE SAM"

Now, I have often wondered why VA, employees have medical insurance. Some say, the Va facility is for Vets. It would seem from a business stand point, cost cutting (Oh, I must say this in the middle here. All the cuts congress is considering, and says must be done. May 2012, congressional Vote, All congressmen get a pension lifetime, well, congress voted to keep their pension, not add it to budget reduction. Just a thought!!!!!) I would like to have their medical plan. Just a passing thought. The American taxpayers have plenty of money-right.

Since, for the last 10 years, the VA, has been caught many times, having too many Vets die in Va, hospitals. Surgeons performing surgeries they are not trained to do, gross incompetence, no one went to jail though. They were just fired that's all. A slap on the hand. After all, We are just Vets. At least now; many VA Hospitals refer out a surgery, that's a positive move. Can you believe I said positive in relation to the VA.

Another policy that changed, and I must compliment the VA, so many Vets were dying, because, if you wanted the VA, to pay for your EMERGENCY ROOM VISIT, you had to have the ambulance first take you to the VA, get a form, then be transported to the nearest hospital. One would think if you go to a VA, hospital, you could get treated. Hard for them to find a heart doctor for what they pay, right. But; many Vets died on the way from VA, because you had to produce your Va ID card they had to fill out a form etc, **heart doctors**

and the American Heart association, says having a heart attack, minutes count, not the VA, but; on the positive side, now you can go straight to the Emergency room, it's the hospital has to notify the VA, within 72 hours. As soon as possible you will be taken to a VA facility, that's bad.

I personally feel the VA, commits fraud every day. By this I mean, in the Va, the budget submitted to Congress, includes all care and associated costs. The VA, requires Vets, to report private insurance, Medicaid, medicare, Tricare all, they do bill your insurance carriers. Some Vets who use the VA, have to pay a co-pay for medicine and treatment. Why, do I feel it's a fraud; it doesn't seem that the many hundreds of thousand vets, seem to reduce the VA's budget? If the VA, is asking for money across the board, why collect. I can't seem to find these allocations in budget reporting of budget request's, so if the taxpayers are paying, reduce the budget, if not the VA, gets money from taxpayers, money from insurance, is this having your cake and eat it to???

Remember, on the cover, I stated and cited the California courts ruling and that Congress has established by law, the VA, is exempt from judicial review.

Now, the VA, has a court, called the United States Court of Appeals for Veteran Claims. That sounds great, but; it is basically an in house court. By that I mean, it does not have a federally appointed **Judge**, because, it does not say" United **States District Court for** Veteran Appeals" and the VA, when this court reaches a decision on a claim appealed pay much attention. They go on their merry crusade of delays. I have been there, much to the same.

Now, hiring in the VA, anyone who has tried will tell you it's a forever process. My center say's there are no job openings. From a business standpoint, why are there 14 people working in there on a daily basis. Jobs are for friends, relatives, etc. Since I'm a veteran my wife could get a job with veteran preference. I don't have insider knowledge. DAH

I have a degree from northwestern UN. Chicago, Il. I have a 3.75 GPA. I can receive a direct appointment without being in the competitive process. Other words I can interview today go to work tomorrow. When I applied, I was offered a job as a janitor. The Veterans admin does not implore Vets to work at the VA. The vast majority of VA, employees is non-vets, does that make sense??????

I apologize for skipping around, so much to point out and ensure that all understand this dictatorship, I have much more, but; for a later book. I'm trying not to make this a 3-4-500 page book.

One of the most famous statements from the VA is; when you claim an injury from service, it must manifest itself to a compensable degree within one year from date of discharge. I can never completely absorb this statement. Reason being, It took many veteran groups, lobbying, to get the Dept. of defense, the chemical company that made agent orange, and the VA, to recognize the DANGERS associated with this disease . The course of this legal battle was 26 years after the U.S., left Vietnam. Earlier this year (2012), the Secretary of the VA, thru the National Health Sciences Committee, added three more, so the process continues as more have different infections, diseases, and symptoms from Agent Orange tropical application. Meaning, this stuff is so bad, that in Vietnam, on Monday, they sprayed, on Thursday, a person could literally; push a 100 yr. old tree over. No vegetation will grow for centuries. And as U.S. Troops, we were directly sprayed with this. Wasn't ask, it was decided, I have a document from the Va's files that says they have the right to experiment with us. I hope someone in the VA, challenges me, I'll pop it out in a heartbeat. Makes me afraid to be vaccinated anymore. No telling what our Government will do to you when you put on a uniform. Just think of the soldiers, put in bunkers at the testing of the atom bomb, when no one knew the effects. They found out the effects when the soldiers were blinded, radiation poisoned etc. etc. etc. What a government we have!!!!

In September2012, I was given a pet scan by the VA, in a rather large hospital. The results were (I have documents) Mastoiditis-infection of the inner ear-very serious, Bone Cancer, which had Matastized, incurable but; treatable (can slow down the progression, but; can't stop it) two other lymph node cancers. I must explain this, I was single, lived alone, new in this city, I have outlived my family, so I'm on my own, by myself. I had a pinched nerve from neck to and through my right arm. Couldn't sleep without constant interruption, every time I moved, I woke up. I called the VA, for a visiting nurse, to reinforce me, to no avail. I sat there for 3 months, no return appointments were scheduled, I was worried, severely stressed, no help, no nothing. After 2 months I finally got the nerve relaxed, moved back to my previous residence. Got an appointment with my Va, provider, she sent my team assignment into outer space. I'm not assigned, so no one picks me up for diabetes monitoring, follow up for cancer, no referrals to the contract oncologist, no any nothing. After 6 weeks, I was assigned to another team, finally was getting help, and didn't really need that much then, I will explain.

When I moved back, I received an immediate appointment with my Oncologist, a renowned Doctor and Author. Performs his own research studies, has his own labs, chemo and radiation facilities. He immediately ordered a bone scan. The results-NEGATIVE, he then ordered a cat-scan with dye, NO CANCER, NO ANYTHING. Finally I received an appointment with the Contract Oncologist at the VA, his look said it all, They mixed me up with another patient. Not the first time. On a 2011, x-ray at the VA, my comp/pen doctor, looked at the scar from my cancer and lung removal, but the x-ray showed me with both lungs, until she called the x-ray room, they finally changed it too mine. Can you imagine the Vet, that is being told he has lost a half a lung. This is not an occasional mix-up, happens all the time. PLEASE READ CHAPTER 3, THE LIST AND AN EXPLANATION OF THE DISEASE WITH Vietnam and gulf war vets Since it is obvious that the VA, got the results mixed up, another veteran is living daily thinking he is alright, meanwhile this bone cancer and Mastoiditis, and 2 other cancers are growing, and he has been told by the VA, he is ok. More than likely he will die before he can get a grip, and the cancers sread beyond saving him. But; I can't get anyone to give me a letter stating it was a mix up. Wonder did they try to find the veteran that actually has these cancers.!!?????

CHAPTER THREE

In this chapter I will outline and discuss the diseases associated with Agent Orange (Vietnam Era), The Gulf War Syndrome (Iraq Conflict) The Navy and marines suffering from Cancer due to Asbestos exposure on our older ships, and military Barracks used but; left over from the World War 2, and Korean conflict.

It is to be a significant factor that in the last 20 years, I have ask every Doctor, that I have been a patient of outside the VA, if they know of the afflictions associated with these, and the response has always been "NO". I have asked of the VA, doctors that I have seen and they also respond "NO". That is mind blowing. The VA does not report these to the New England Medical Journal, or any other source outside of the VA, itself. I OFTEN WONDER 'WHY'

I always if seeing a doctor for the first time bring a list for them to review. Most doctors have expressed amazement at the fact they have not been made aware of the afflictions. Any logical person would want to disseminate this to the medical community and among its own doctors. Maybe the VA feels it's immune. They have Congress behind them, and immune from prosecution and The United States Court's cannot review or rule on the them, because of the private enterprise operating with U.S. Tax Payers money!!!!!

Should the VA, be subjected to and adhere to the Courts, be subjected to lawsuits for malpractice, the care and less Veterans would die as a result of negligence on the behalf of the VA. Of all the news media, newspaper articles of abuse of veterans, veterans dying at VA hospitals in Masses, NO ONE HAS YET BEEN PROSECUTED, JAILED, OR ANY OTHER MEASURE THAN FIRED. To this author, I personally find it appalling, a thumb by the VA, which it will do as it pleases, when it pleases, and no one will say different. The diseases that are periodically added cause a backlog of claims. Should the VA, do what's right and proper, and come out with all this in the beginning, the backlogs would not choke the VA, but; it gives them the leverage to go to congress, ask for more money, hire more people. The VA has people tripping over each other, and still nothing gets done, oh, I should clarify that, it does get done; it just takes endless unnecessary years to accomplish.

If it is permissible, I must render an apology to readers. Only a person who has dealt with the VA, can understand what a Vet, has to endure. I'm not on a vendetta, just attempting to bring awareness of a ROGUE agency, and hoping people of America, will understand the plight of Veterans. We did offer our life to our country, and when suffering wounds in action, we are at the absolute mercy of the VA.!!!!

The LIST;

1. Chloracne(must incur within 1 year of exposure to Agent Orange)
   It must be noted here-It took the U.S. Government and the chemical manufacturer 26 years after Vietnam, to admit these diseases. It has an immediate and long term effect. Its incubation period can range from day 1, thru 30 years, and it comes from the inside out.
2. Non-Hodgkin's lymphoma. (A group of malignant tumors CANCERS that affect the lymph glands and other tissue. Fatal
3. Soft tissue sarcoma((A group of different kinds malignant tumors(CANCER) that arise from body tissues such as muscle, fat, blood, and lymph vessels. Occur in the soft tissues of the body.
4. Hodgkin 's disease (A Malignant lymphoma (cancer) characterized by progressive enlargement of the lymph nodes, liver, and spleen, and by progressive anemia.
5. Porphyria catenae tread(a disorder of liver and by thinning and blistering of the skin in sun exposed area's)
6. Multiple Myeloma (A Cancer Of specific bone marrow cells that is Characterized by bone marrow tumors in various bones of the body.
7. Respiratory Cancers (Cancers of the lung, larynx, trachea, and bronchus.
8. Prostate Cancer(self-explanatory
9. Peripheral neuropathy (A nervous system condition that causes muscle weakness, numbness and tingling.
10. Diabetes Mellitus- both kinds
11. Chronic Lymphocytic Leukemia (A slow progressing disease.

IN CHILDREN AND WOMEN VIETNAM VETERANS- Spina Bifada- A neural tube birth defect

Other disabilities in children of women Vietnam vets the VA, has not expounded upon.

August 2010 3 new diseases added, after 40 years-you would say-kind of late-huh

Hairy (or B cell leukemia-slow growing cancer of the blood-deadly

Ischemic Heart disease (reduced blood flow to the heart

Parkinson's disease-self explanatory

All these are listed on the VA website-VA.gov.

I can only hope and I do pray, someone looks at this in stark amazement and finally start complaining to congress and the senators, how could the United States of America, do this to it's own servicemen and women, and get away with it????? How can the congress allow the VA, to hide behind the law, and since all have been ordered into combat zones, then treated the way we are, in America, and no help with this astronomical machine called, The Veterans Administration??????

Now to the gulf war, it hasn't yet been concluded what our soldiers have been afflicted with. What a stark realization from the VA!!!!!

Ask the soldiers, sailors, airmen and Marines. Mustard Gas and anthrax. For political reasons, no one is willing to admit this real happening. Here are the results from the VA and pentagon records;

Troops deployed in Persian Gulf-696,628

Believed to have been exposed to Chemical agents-100,000

Troops who received treatment-250,000

Those who received Botulism vaccine-8,000

Received Anthrax Vaccine-150,000

Exposed to depleted Uranium-436,000- Did you know and can you realize how this is being studied 12 years after, and how it's been downplayed???? Exposed to Depleted Uranium, that is not to be taken lightly!!!! But; the VA, is!!!

Our sailors by the thousands have been exposed to Asbestos, aboard our ships. You would think that in the past 30 years the Navy and Marine departments would have known this sooner, rather than later. But; it's only the government and service members are just that-WHO CARES IS THE ATTITUDE OF THE DAY1111

Side note: As of September 30, 2010, there were 22.7, million Veterans Living

In reading this it is intended to reach out, hope the people of this country can see how the Veterans have fought, performed their duty, and then be treated so very poorly by a dictatorship form of Government.

Please read on to chapter 4.

CHAPTER FOUR

In this chapter I will outline the Claims process, in and out, in detail.

When a veteran first files a claim with the VA, it will be sent to the Regional Office governing that region.

All supporting documents the veteran has should be attached. At that point sometime within months or longer in most cases the Regional Office will either approve or deny the claim. In most cases this office will order an exam by the dreaded compensation and pension examiner. This nurse practitioner or doctor may or may not order additional tests. It's solely at that person's discretion. From the time that person walks out to the waiting area and calls your name, you are judged by how you were sitting in the chair, when you stood up, how you walked, how you sat in the chair in their office, how you got on the exam table, every movement is judged. Also, the examiner, will check you over, and regardless of previous tests, and remember, most injuries are internal. Without looking inside, and no previous experience with you, and not reviewing your VA, doctors notes and tests, render a decision of your claims. I have been told several times by the C/P, examiner, no discussion, answer yes or no, a couple of days later when I went to release of records, and obtained a copy, I came home sat down and read this report. The VA, as I stated earlier, by doctors' orders, I was put in a wheelchair. The ability of my movements precludes working. The examiner noted I was functional and capable of working with no limitations. In an earlier chapter I discussed the problems with my physical abilities; I'm embarrassed and won't go into them again. I'm not an idle person, have had to admit a lot of things I used to do, and cannot perform now, it's hard when you have been active all your life.

This should be performed by your VA, doctor. In my opinion. He knows you, treats you, and has ordered exams, tests, etc. But: the c/p, again in my opinion, is by doctors, whom you do not know, and has no idea of what is going on inside your body, and really, cannot be a team doctor; because of most of them has an attitude.

This is where the VA, puts you behind the eight ball, and you begin a long arduous journey of attempting to overcome this report. The second issue, some diseases have developed thru the years that are associated with service, but; even a presumptive issue, the VA, is stuck on this statement and I quote" did this manifest to a compensable degree within one year after separation from the service" and this one, "did it heal within 2 years from onset after discharge. Often I wonder if someone in the VA reads their own statements. If you served in Vietnam, you are by VA, policy and rules, considered as presumptively exposed to Agent Orange. Secondly, it took 26 years to admit by the Government this was used. Sounds like the right and left are missing each other. Vietnam, ended in 1972, in 2010, the Secretary of the VA, adds 3 new illnesses, but; did they manifest to a compensable degree within one year. That's what they say. I still at times shake my head, but; that's the Government. It is an issue which we as veterans, have to overcome.

Now, after 1 day to 2 years, you will be approved or denied. Bet you can guess which one. In this case you will have to file a NOTICE OF DISAGREEMENT, state why you disagree with their decision. As with most veterans, my terminology, we use the double standard. When in a VA, hospital you will see veterans carrying huge bags of pills. The VA will pill you up, cure you NO. The medicines are old. I have to cut some of my pills, when I do, they crumble, and I get a half and the rest I have to throw away. So, I know its old medicine. You have to watch the VA. My insulin needles, I know that I fill the needle with 40 units of insulin, that's about half the syringe, I normally receive. When I start filling the syringe then I notice it's a different gauge, and it takes most of the syringe. I normally take a 40mg pill; I will receive an 80mg and instructed to cut it in half. ALWAYS when dealing with the VA, on medication compare new to old. Never assume. You would be surprised how many times you will receive medication that is not prescribed to you. I received a refill of insulin pens, no needles. When I called the pharmacy, I was told impossible, they always send needles, and I had to buy a box, until I was on an appointment and told my doctor, he then prescribed the needles.

Ok, now your claim has been denied. You have filed your NOD, with this you should file all documents and tests and outline them in detail. State what they are, the diagnosis, how it affects you, and what limitations it causes and how it affects your work and daily functions.

Most veterans including this author utilize private doctors. That way you won't have something affecting you or killing you, and I mean that deliberate and intentionally. The VA, has caused upon me missed diagnosis, and diagnosed cancers, that I have received NO care or treatment...When I was diagnosed with Coronary heart disease. I received NO medications or treatment from 1998, until I had a 4 valve bypass in 2005. Include your private doctor's tests and medical notes and his diagnosis treatment orders. Go to Title 18, C.F.R., this is the law and rules of the VA.

When you read Title 18, you will readily see how the VA, rates claims. Many Veterans I have spoken to, have no idea and have never reviewed the procedures, contained within this reference. This is most important to understand how they review and rate. You can then tailor your response according to their procedures. On a leg. The VA, rating system does not rate the leg as a whole. It's the upper. Foreleg, knee. Foot and toes.

The same applies when you apply for a VA, job. They have now instead of the SF 171, they now utilize the resume. Here again, a general resume will not help you in obtaining employment with any government agency. They use the standard of KSA, (knowledge, skills, and abilities.) Therefore you will have to tailor your resume to fit the position to which you are applying.

While you are in and reviewing Title 18, read the section governing the Board of Veteran appeals. How they function and what's required. You can, if severely injured, ask for expedited review, when in a hardship situation. Most of the time, the BVA, will remand back to the regional office. It says their decisions are to be expedited. Don't believe that in a heartbeat. They will normally send your records to the appeals management center. This is the ultimate delay, lay around records, my last remand stayed at the appeals center, for 2 and a half years, I finally wrote and demanded make a decision. Either approve or disapprove. While your records are there, you cannot file any additional claims, because they have your records, and the regional office cannot access your files. The VA, still today utilizes paper records. Yes, that's what I said, paper records. You would think with the advent of computers, all would on computer. That would make the VA, work and process claims more efficiently. So, your records get mailed thru the mails. Once your records arrive at any VA, they must go thru screening. You will find it takes 2 weeks to a month to get an acknowledgement from the VA, that your corresponded has been received. The VA, in other words is still archaic in this modern world. Should all be computerized, exchanging e-mail request to expedite your claim, it's all paper. I have about 75 lbs. of papers here in a 5 drawer file cabinet and collecting more each week. The VA, will paper work you to death.

The claims, this will shock you at the staggering numbers. In order to handle the number of claims, this is the system the VA, employs. File claim with regional office. Deny claim, appeal to board of veteran appeals. Remand to appeals management center, delay there, send on back to regional office, rework and deny, start process all over again, now after board of veteran appeals, should the board decide against the veteran, appeal to the US Court of Veteran Appeals, here it takes about 4 years. One hell of a system, well designed and in place. You may have answered the call to duty, fought in the wars, when you apply for your just due, guess what you get;

The Veterans Administration.

From the gulf war, here is a breakdown of the claims, as of 2000, Gulf theater veterans filing claims, 249, and 810. Approved-192,024, denied-26410-pending, 31,376. With Iraq, still going, Afghanistan, and the new additions of Agent Orange causes, the backlog, is tremendous. You could be unemployable, and wait 10 years. Now, in 2012, with budget cuts, so many new veterans, the backlog is over 560,000, over 125 days old.

The VA, is going to have to change and rapidly. But; I can guarantee it won't. No one there cares, gives a grave concern and Congress, and is trying to get re-elected.

On Memorial Day, I watched the President, and after the ceremony, people and dignitaries were talking on stage. As everyone left the stage, the only one on camera, walking around the stage looking lost, no friends, was, guess who, The Secretary of Veteran Affairs. I thought that was so funny. He was looking like, where did everybody go????? Does that tell you something????

The VA, to be honest, is overwhelmed. The upper management and the tier level of executives, sub-level, are many, but; planning, execution, and outright foresight does leave one to wonder, where was the prior planning??

The old practice of denials, and choking the BVA, has got to cease. As with the emails obtained in the 9th Circuit Court, when the VA, at lower levels, a regional, Office, was told, by an upper level manager, they were approving too many PTSD, claims. It thusly appears the VA, doesn't want to streamline its process, but; continue to choke the system with endless denials, delaying the inevitable that eventually it will be approved. The claims meet the criteria, but; let's pass it around for a couple years. I'm not being negative, but; I watch the process, and on the surface, that's the way it appears, in all honesty. The VA, can and will and does, spin you around the gambit of its system for 5 years, and start you all over again. This is a well-defined and structured system, and many veterans just give up. I feel, that's the purpose. In a court case, the VA can delay you inevitably. Many veterans have filed cases against the VA. I'm happy they have the money. Because, when you speak with an attorney, and you say VA, the price tag starts high and only goes higher. Rather than grant a claim, they will hire only the best, and fight you like it was their last dollar.

For the military service member leaving the service, after combat, the fight he or she is about to encounter is enough to give you PTSD. I have a degree in Business. But; the way this process is handled, on the surface, a definite lack of proper planning, coupled with poor management, a Secretary, whom doesn't mind the store, uses his travel to the fullest level, because, on a travel voucher, he does make extra money, given the per diem rates. Staying in ultra-nice hotels, having fancy dinners. Again I personally feel, he should stay, oversee his department and make effort to get the ball rolling, manage and execute, not travel and ignore.

This has become a short book, but; did not want to make it long and boring. I sincerely hope those who read, have gained insight and knowledge. Perhaps enough to alert your elected representatives, your dismay over the handling of the many hundreds of thousand veterans who have to ONCE AGAIN ENDURE TO THE END.

This author offers his prayers and many Thanks too everyone.

CHAPTER FIVE

In this chapter to lend credibility to the things I have stated, I have included actual case files and literature I have received from the VA. I have blanked out name address and case numbers, for obvious reasons. There have been many times when receiving letters and case decisions from the VA; I wonder if they read what they write. When they tell me that here again my claim is being remanded again, and in the same paragraph tell me how many times and since 1998, this has been an ongoing issue, do they read this?? Is this an ongoing process??? YES.

This goes from regional office, denied to me, I must gather all documents, copy, write an answer called notice of disagreement, send to the board of veteran appeals, wait 2 or 3 years, they say it has defaults and must be perfected by the regional office, and another 2 years, the regional office again denies, when it is obvious that I'm entitled, but; it is easier to deny. And the whole thing starts all over again. This is the VA, way of doing business. This is what I'm attempting to bring awareness to, the American public is being brain washed by the VA, press releases when the VA, still has not complied with their own statements. What a federal beaucratic agency. This is what the veterans of our country go through on a daily basis. Yes, we put our lives on the line. But; when you are messed up, crippled, don't ask our government for your just promises and help. You have no more need to the government. So, then you are discarded as so much trash.

I have sent president Obama, emails. He says he answers all. Maybe it's because he didn't say when he would answer. Still waiting, 3 months now. I written and explained the plight of what the VA, is doing to veterans. The speaker of the house Boehner, NO RESPONSE!!! All congressmen in committee chairs, NO RESPONSE!! Senators, forget it!!!! They want you young, ready to fight. When you leave you get the VETERANS ADMINISTRATION. WHAT A REWARD1111

Please read the following cases, make up your own mind. Should you feel as I, and over 22 million veterans, please, comment, write, talk to your representative in congress. Ask what you are doing to our veterans, Please...

Thank you, all who read and respond, I welcome good or bad feedback, and wish all, happiness, be safe, and please remember, GOD is good.

BOARD OF VETERANS' APPEALS

~~Department of Veterans Affairs~~

WASHINGTON, DC 20420

IN THE APPEAL OF   C 24 ~~████~~

~~████████████████████~~

                                    SEP 1 6 2011

DOCKET NO. 00-13 ~~██~~   )   DATE

)

)

On appeal from the
Department of Veterans Affairs Regional Office in ~~████████~~s, ~~████████~~

THE ISSUES

1. Entitlement to service connection for a right shoulder disorder with arthritis.

2. Entitlement to service connection for an enlarged gland disorder (claimed as a lump in the throat and neck), to include as due to herbicide (Agent Orange) exposure.

3. Entitlement to a total disability rating based on individual unemployability (TDIU) due to service-connected disabilities.

(The issues of entitlement to a waiver of recovery of overpayment of pension / compensation benefits in the original calculated amounts of $6,472 and $12,144, to include the preliminary issue of the validity of the debts will be addressed in a separate decision).

WITNESS AT HEARING ON APPEAL

The Veteran

IN THE APPEAL OF   ('

DOCKET NO.   DATE

I

On appeal from the
Department of Veterans Affairs Regional Office in

["HE ISSUES

1. Entitlement to service connection for a right shoulder disorder with arthritis.

2. Entitlement to service connection for an enlarged gland disorder (claimed as a lump in the throat and neck), to include as due to herbicide (Agent Orange) exposure.

3. Entitlement to a total disability rating based on indiv idual unempioyability (I DIU) due to service-connected disabilities.

(The issues of entitlement to a waiver of recovery of overpayment of pension / compensation benefits in the original calculated amounts of   and . to include the preliminary issue of the validity of the debts will be addressed in a separate decision).

WITNESS AT HEARING ON APPEAL

1 he Veteran

Court. In fact, the specific Agent Orange residual issues that were addressed in the Court's February 2005 Memorandum Decision are no longer before the Board.

:i March J^fe the Veteran presented testimony at a hearing before the undersigned Veterans Law Judge at the RO (Fravel Board hearing).

Finally, the Board notes that the Veteran was previously represented by the Texas Veterans Commission. However, in July 2006 he submitted a document which indicated that he had moved from J^nMatiHHMmti. Accordingly, he revoked their power of attorney. When asked about any new representative authorized to act an his behalf, the Veteran responded "none. Veteran only." It was also noted at [he March 2011 hearing that the Veteran was unrepresented. Therefore, the Veteran has revoked his appointment of the Texas Veterans Commission as his accredited representative. *See* 38 C.F.R. $ 14.63 Hf)(1) (2010). He has not since appointed another representative.

The appeal is REMANDED to the RO via the Appeals Management Center (AMC). in Washington. DC. VA will notify the appellant if further action is required.

.

REMAND

First, at the March 2011 hearing the Veteran stated that he was receiving disability benefits from the Social Security Administration (SSA) since 2007. *See* hearing testimony at page 16. In addition, the Veteran submitted a March 2009 authorization (VA Form 21-4142) for VA to secure these SSA disability records. Nonetheless, his SSA records are not on file and must be obtained before deciding these claims since these records may specifically concern the particular conditions at issue. 38 U.S.C.A. § 5103A(c)(3); 38 C.F.R. § 3.159(c)(2). VA has a duty to make reasonable efforts to assist a claimant to obtain evidence necessary to substantiate the claim. 38 U.S.C.A. § 5103A(a)(1); 38 C.F.R. § 3.159(c). Although disability determinations by the SSA are not controlling on VA. they are pertinent to the adjudication of a claim for VA benefits and VA has a duty to assist the Veteran in gathering these records. *Voerth* v. *West.* 13 Vet. App. 117. 121 (1999);

opriate action must be handled in an expeditious manner. *See* 38   U.S.C.A. 5109B, 7112 (West
   Supp. 2010).

-- A\^\^£\\ _____

A. BRYANT Veterans Law Judge. Board of Veterans'

Appeals

I Inder 38 U.S.C.A. § 7252 (West 2002). only a decision of the Board of Veterans' \ppeals
is appealable to the United States Court of Appeals for Veterans Claims. This remand is in
the nature of a preliminary order and does not constitute a decision of the Board on the
merits of your appeal. 38 C.F.R. § 20.1100(b) (2010).

You Blocked Veteran from an appeal
to the USCVA, now you must
make a decision as to the merits
and failure of Repeated Remands
which are a result of paperwork
playing !

BOARD OF VETERANS' APPEALS

WASHINGTON, DC 20420

IN THE APPEAL OF

DOCKET NO.   ) DATE)

On appeal from the Department of Veterans Affairs Regional Office in
Houston, Texas

THE ISSUES

1. Entitlement to service connection for right submandibular lymphadenopathy with
an asymmetrically enlarged right submandibular gland, to include as secondary to
herbicide exposure.

2. Entitlement to service connection for osteoarthritic change involving the right
acromioclavicular joint.

3. Entitlement to a total disability rating based on individual unemployability due to
service-connected disabilities (TDIU).

4. Entitlement to waiver of overpayment of disability compensation benefits in the
amount of $6,472.

REPRESENTATIVE

Appellant represented by:aTTORNEY FOR THE BOARD

Counsel

Radiology Reports

Exm Date: DEC 02, 2011@09:27
Req Phys: ██████FRANCISCO A

Pat Loc: ████████████████████████
Img Loc: ████████ PET/CT
Service: Unknown

(Case 2241 COMPLETE) PET/CT SKULL-MID THIGH   (NM   Detailed) CPT:78815
        Reason for Study: See Clinical History

(Case 2243 COMPLETE) F-18 FDG, UP TO 45 MCI PER STUDY (NM   Detailed) CPT:A9552

(Case 2245 COMPLETE) FUROSEMIDE (LASIX) UP TO 20 MG   (NM   Detailed) CPT:J1940
        Pharmaceutical: FUROSEMIDE 10MG/ML INJ , 10mg

(Case 2246 CANCELLE) NM ORAL CONTRAST   (NM   Detailed) CPT:A9698

   Clinical History:
     Age: 65 Weight: 201 lb [91.4 kg] (11/29/2011 08:12) Height: 72 in
     [182.9 cm] (10/31/2011 09:50)

     Approved Indication: 5. Lung Cancer Sub Indication: (A) Diagnosis
     Size of Lesion (cm): RIGHT HUMEORUS METASTATIC DISEASE — *Bone Cancer*
     NOTE: Lesion size must be above 1cm ***Other:

     Clinical history/reason for exam: IN 2007 HAD A LUNG CANCER
     REMOVE RIGHT UPPER LOBECTOMY, CONTSINUE BEING SMOKER, AND NOW
     WITH SEVERE PAIN RIGHT HUMEROUS, AND THIS SEEN TO BE METASTATIC
     DISEASE TO THE BONE. REQUESTING A TOTAL BODY PET/SPIRAL CT SCAN

     REQUIRED for all Female Patients: **Urine pregnancy test required
     for all under age 55 without serilization
            Pregnant: N/A
            Breast Feeding: N/A
            HX of hysterectomy or tubal ligation: N/A
            Urine Pregnancy test ordered: N/A

     Diabetic: Yes **PET scan may be cancelled if FBS over 300

     Claustrophobic: No Radiation Treatment within past 2 months? No

     Can patient lie down for 30 minutes? Yes Can patient raise arms
     over head for 30 minutes? Yes

     Is patient allergic to Lasix? No

   Report Status: Verified   Date Reported: DEC 02, 2011

 **Department of Veterans Affairs**

 FROM: 9/3/11   8 months - nothing

83 (**April 16, 2012**)

In Reply Refer To:

TRAVIS D CRAWFORD

File Number:
24 -
PAYEE NO 00

We are still processing your application for COMPENSATION. We apologize for the delay.
You will be notified upon completion of processing. If you need to contact us, be sure to
show the file number and full name of the veteran.

If your mailing address is different than that shown above, please advise us of your new
mailing address. You should notify us immediately of any changes in your mailing address.

If you reside in the Continental United States, Alaska, Hawaii, Guam, the Northern Marianas,
or Puerto Rico, you may contact VA with questions and receive free help by calling our toll-
free number 1-800-827-1000 (for hearing impaired TDD 1-800-829-4833). From American
Samoa you may dial toll free 684-699-3730.

Note: TDD phone number 1-800-829-4833 does not work for callers residing in Guam and
the Northern Marianas.

S. KELLY

VETERANS SERVICE CENTER MANAGER

 *HAVE Been Since 1999.*

Radiology Reports

CT CONTRAST ONLY SOFT TISSUE NECK

[handwritten: Hey, had cancer, can you look for that !!]

Proc Ord: CT NECK SOFT TISSUE W/CONT
Exm Date: NOV 09, 2011@08:32
Req Phys: QDISHO, ██████

Pat Loc: ████████████████ O (Req'g
Img Loc: CT ███
Service: Unknown

(Case 1126 COMPLETE) CT CONTRAST ONLY SOFT TISSUE NECK(CT   Detailed) CPT:70491
   Contrast Media : Ionic Iodinated
   Reason for Study: r/o mass

(Case 1127 COMPLETE) LOCM-CT   (CT   Detailed) CPT:Q9967
   Contrast Media : Ionic Iodinated

Clinical History:
   h/o Lf neck tumor resection per remote data. c/o pain and
   ??swelling in Rt upper neck

Report Status: Verified

Date Reported: NOV 09, 2011
Date Verified: NOV 09, 2011

Verifier E-Sig:/ES/ANIL K. MALIK, MD

Report:
   CT neck with contrast. No comparison

After intravenous injection of 100 cc of Visipaque 320
intravenous contrast, 3.8 mm thick contiguous axial images were
obtained from skull base to upper chest.

No discrete sizable mass lesion is seen in the right or left
aspect of the neck. Surgical clips are noted in the suprasternal
notch, of indeterminate nature. There are sternotomy wires.
Short axis subcentimeter sized mediastinal and bilateral cervical
lymph nodes are nonspecific. Bilateral parotid and submandibular
salivary glands are normal. No definite pharyngeal or laryngeal
mucosal mass lesion is seen. Thyroid gland is normal. There are
vascular calcifications. There is cervical spondylotic changes.
Visualized brain parenchyma is normal. No sinusitis. There is
bilateral partial mastoiditis. Patient is status post ACDF C3-4.

Impression:
   1. No discrete sizable neck mass is seen. 2. Status post ACDF
and sternotomy. 3. Bilateral partial mastoiditis. Please see
above description.

[handwritten left margin: Didn't mention 3-10mm nodes inf/Lung - low at on Lymph gland. Surgical diffuse's Papers, For Magna Frade Cam!]

[handwritten right margin: ? What is this / I have for years NO AIRFl out of my Sinus]

PATIENT NAME AND ADDRESS (Mechanical imprinting, if available)

█████████████
9250 DEAN ROAD APT 412
███████████████

VISTA Electronic Medical Documentation

Printed at ████████████ VAMC

 **RIVER**
SLEEP CENTER

, M.D.
, M.D.

Letter of Medical Necessity

06-07-2007

Patient Name:	▇▇▇▇▇▇▇.
Date of Birth:	10/17/1946
Physician:	Dr. R.▇▇
Equipment Required:	E0601 CPAP Machine, A7037 Tubing, A7038 Filters, A7036 Chinstrap, E0562 Heated Humidifier, A7035 Headgear, A7034 Nasal Mask

Dear Insurance Carrier/Claims Processing Unit,

The above listed patient has been diagnosed with Obstructive Sleep Apnea Syndrome (327.23), a condition in which the muscles that control the tongue and palate relax too much during sleep and block the upper airway, preventing breathing. This disorder can be life threatening if left untreated. Therefore a prescription for the purchase of a CPAP airway management system has been recommended to treat this disorder and its symptoms.

CPAP therapy is considered the best available and most cost-effective therapy for OSAS. It provides an alternative to tracheostomy, or to the less radical uvulopalatopharyngoplasty surgery, for this patient whose disorder, if left untreated, is potentially life threatening. To achieve the mandatory treatment, this equipment has been prescribed and is medically required to treat the disorder of Obstructive Sleep Apnea Syndrome. The typical duration of need for this equipment is lifetime. Based on this fact the outright purchase of the CPAP device and all equipment / supplies is deemed medically necessary.

A prescription for the simultaneous use of heated humidification is recommended to prevent the side effects of nasal dryness, mucosal dehydration, rhinitis or sinusitis. If not addressed, these side effects can lead to non-compliance and ineffective treatment.

Due to the serious nature of this letter I am convinced that you do not wish to have the liability of this patient, this patient's diagnosis and treatment to rest upon you related to hesitant approval and slow handling. In your prompt professional consideration I would ask that you please expedite accordingly.

Sincerely,

Phone ▇▇▇▇▇▇   Web: www.▇▇▇▇▇▇▇▇   Fax: 3▇▇▇▇▇▇

```
              stable
          HTN
              well controlled
          Back/leg pain
              followed locally & will discuss pain management with that provider as
          he would like to avoid pain management requirements here
              Alzheimers          Still not Receving treatment ! Getting it
                  discussed that medication likely will only slow progression    PRIvately.
                  encouraged to seek out support groups for helpful tools, etc
          OSA/restless legs
              stable

          MED RECON:
              Medication Reconciliation:
                Patient was asked the following questions:
                  What VA meds are you prescribed?
                    Are you taking them as prescribed?
                  What NON-VA meds are you prescribed?
                    Are you taking them as prescribed?
                  What over the counter and or herbals are you taking?

              All medications were reconciled; medications added/deleted/adjusted as
              needed in CPRS; and a printout of active/pending medications was given
              to the patient.

              reschedule 4 months   NO ACA due to dementia

      /es/ ████████████
      CRNP
      Signed: 10/22/2008 11:09

      10/22/2008 ADDENDUM                          STATUS: COMPLETED


      Note to vet regarding lab results
              HGBA1c not at goal  has increased since last checked here   Recommend he
      f/u with provider locally who provides medication
              Platelets low  asked to let PCP know this as well

      For 4 month followup needs diabetes panel with lipids, cbc, psa

      /es/ ████████████
      CRNP
      Signed: 10/22/2008 15:32
```

Board of Veterans' Appeals
Washington DC 20420

Date: 10/19/99

In Reply Refer To: ⬛⬛⬛⬛⬛

3rd time now 2 more times — 3 yrs waiting in between

Dear Appellant:

Your appeal was received at the Board of Veterans Appeals (Board) and was returned to the docket. If you are represented by a veterans service organization, your file will be referred to your representative for the preparation and submission of a brief in support of your case. If you have requested a personal hearing before a member of the Board, you, or your representative, will be contacted to schedule such a hearing. Under the Boards Rules of Practice most communications concerning your appeal will be sent to your representative if you are represented by a veterans service organization, attorney or agent.

Since your appeal was previously remanded for additional action by the originating agency, we will act on your case before any new appeal that is received by the Board. Despite the priority status of your case, it still may take some time before we can give you a decision. A delay at this time could be due to any number of matters, including its complexity, whether a personal hearing or a question involving representation is involved, and whether further development of the evidence or record is required. Please be assured that your case will be acted upon as expeditiously as practicable.

The Board has employees available to answer your questions about the status of your case at the Board. Please feel free to contact us at (202) 565-5436. The Boards hours of operation are 8:00 a.m. to 4:30 p.m., Eastern time, Monday through Friday. Any questions about factual or legal matters involved in your appeal should be directed to your representative, if you have one.

The letter that your local VA regional office sent to you when it forwarded your VA file to us includes important information about restrictions on sending the Board new evidence about your case and on requesting a hearing at the Board or appointing or changing your representative. Please review that information carefully before taking any of those actions.

We have enclosed two pamphlets. The thin pamphlet contains the customer service standards we have pledged to meet. The other pamphlet provides answers to the most commonly asked questions about how the appeal system works. We hope you find these pamphlets informative and helpful.

Sincerely yours,

C. Joe

for Nancy D. Stackhouse
Director, Administrative Service (0141)
By Direction of the Chairman

Enclosures (2)

ANOTHER Remand!

38 U.S.C. § 5109A : US Code - Section 5109A: Revision of decisions on grounds of clear and unmistakable error

Search 38 U.S.C. § 5109A : US Code - Section 5109A: Revision of decisions on grounds of clear and unmistakable error

- Search by Keyword or Citation

[ ] Search

(a) A decision by the Secretary under this chapter is subject to revision on the grounds of clear and unmistakable error. If evidence establishes the error, the prior decision shall be reversed or revised.

(b) For the purposes of authorizing benefits, a rating or other adjudicative decision that constitutes a reversal or revision of a prior decision on the grounds of clear and unmistakable error has the same effect as if the decision had been made on the date of the prior decision.

(c) Review to determine whether clear and unmistakable error exists in a case may be instituted by the Secretary on the Secretary's own motion or upon request of the claimant.

(d) A request for revision of a decision of the Secretary based on clear and unmistakable error may be made at any time after that decision is made.

(e) Such a request shall be submitted to the Secretary and shall be decided in the same manner as any other claim.

[Notes]

38 U.S.C. § 5109B : US Code - Section 5109B: Expedited treatment of remanded claims

Search 38 U.S.C. § 5109B : US Code - Section 5109B: Expedited treatment of remanded claims

- Search by Keyword or Citation

[   ] [Search]

The Secretary shall take such actions as may be necessary to
provide for the expeditious treatment by the appropriate regional
office of the Veterans Benefits Administration of any claim that is
remanded to a regional office of the Veterans Benefits
Administration by the Board of Veterans' Appeals.

[Notes]

« Prev	Up
Revision of decisions on grounds of clear and unmistakable error	Claims

VA, NEVER DOES This!
no one to MAKe them.
C.D, author

Printed in the United States
By Bookmasters